SWEYN FORKBEARD:

THE VIKING WHO WOULD BE KING

Angela Garcia

Cover image of Sweyn Forkbeard from an architectural element in Swansea Guild Hall, Swansea, Wales (Completed 1934), by L.M. Perry (LM Perry at en.wikipedia) Transferred from en.wikipedia to Commons., Public Domain:

https://commons.wikimedia.org/w/index.php?curid=1059706

Copyright © 2017 by Angela D. Garcia

All rights reserved.

ISBN-13: 978-1973971320
ISBN-10: 1973971321

Contents

1 Sweyn Who? 3

2 Sweyn's World 6

3 Sweyn's Viking Heritage 9

4 Sweyn's Father 12

5 Sweyn the Son of Harald 15

6 Sweyn the King of Denmark 17

7 Sweyn the Viking King 20

8 What Happened in the Year 1000? 22

9 Sweyn Forkbeard and Elthelred the Unready 26

10 Sweyn the King of England, Finally! 30

11 Sweyn's Son Knut 32

12 How Do We Know? 35

    Bibliography 37

1
Sweyn Who?

Everyone loves a hero. Heroic stories can teach us great lessons about life. This story is not about a hero. In today's world, Sweyn Forkbeard would probably be called a terrorist. He was one of the many men throughout history who spent his life using force to gain control over large groups of people.

Even though Sweyn was not a hero, except to those who fought with him, there are many lessons to be learned from his life and the lives of others like him. Let's find out about Sweyn Forkbeard.

Sweyn Forkbeard was King of Denmark from 985 CE to 1014 CE. Forkbeard was not his real last name, but a nickname, because of the way he wore his beard parted in the middle. His real name was Sweyn Haraldson, which meant he was the son of Harald.

Sweyn's Father was Harald Gormsson, the son of Gorm. Sweyn's father and grandfather were kings of Denmark too. They also had nicknames. His father was called Harald Bluetooth, and his grandfather was called Gorm the Old. Can you imagine why they might have been given those funny names?

When Sweyn was alive, just like today, many of the royal families throughout Europe were related to each other. Some very old history books say that Sweyn's grandmother or great grandmother was a daughter of Ethelred the First. Ethelred was once a king of England. Not very many people today remember Ethelred the first, but they remember his famous brother who ruled after Ethelred died. His name was Alfred the Great.

Unfortunately, we cannot be sure if Sweyn Forkbeard was really related to a king of England in any way. There are very few ancient records about the ancestors of Danish kings, and some of those are not very easy to figure out, even for Danish historians. However, it is an interesting thing to think about, especially after you have read the story of Sweyn Forkbeard's life.

Just like Ethelred the First, not many people today know about Sweyn Forkbeard, but he played a very important part in the history of Europe. His life affected thousands of people, for better and for worse. He was brave, bold, and ambitious. His name inspired terror and admiration. Very few people in King Sweyn's part of the world would have said, "Sweyn who?"

2
Sweyn's World

Sweyn Forkbeard was born in Denmark, about 965 CE. At that time the people of Norway, Sweden, and Denmark shared a similar language and culture. People from Denmark are called Danes. Sweyn was a Dane.

Denmark is made up of Jutland, a peninsula north of Germany, and hundreds of surrounding islands of various sizes. It covers an area smaller than the American state of West Virginia. When Sweyn was alive, the boundary between Germany and Denmark was clearly marked by the Danevirk. The Danevirk was a series of embankments and fort-like walls that helped protect the Danes from land-based attacks.

Many Danes in Sweyn's world were farmers, but many of those farmers were very poor. They were poor because Danish farms were shrinking in size. How can a farm shrink? Danish law said that a father had to leave a portion of his land to each one of his sons. If his sons had sons, they had to leave a portion of their land to each of their sons, and so on.

Very few Danes knew how to read or write. They had no schools and no libraries. Danish writing was in the form of runes which were symbols made of straight lines carved on stone, wood, coins, and jewelry. The word rune means "mystery" or "secret." When you cannot read, all writing is like a secret code.

The Danes were excellent wood workers and metal smiths. They used their talents to create some of the most beautiful and seaworthy ships in their part of the world. Those ships were able to sail through shallow or deep waters, which meant the Danes could easily travel almost anywhere they wanted to go.

With the North Sea on the north and west sides of Denmark, the Baltic Sea to the east-- as well as many small lakes, rivers, fiords, and marshes on the peninsula-- the Danes made the water part of their everyday life. They used it as a source of food, a method of transportation, and a convenient battleground.

3
Sweyn's Viking Heritage

Some Danes called themselves Vikings. Viking means "sea raider." The Vikings were a lot like pirates. Like pirates, they were hungry for silver and gold, as well as anything that could be carried away. They also wanted more land for their sons and grandsons. Many Vikings were from Norway and Sweden as well. Sweyn became a Viking when he grew up, just like his father before him.

Vikings got the land and treasure they wanted by raiding the countries around them. For about three hundred years, the towns and monasteries of Europe lived in constant fear of the sea raiders. The people of those lands called the Vikings heathens, pagans, foreigners, and northmen. "From the fury of the Northmen, O Lord, deliver us," they would pray.

Christians in many countries were terrified of the Vikings, not just because of the fighting and looting. Some Christians believed that the bible book of Revelation was speaking of the Vikings when it said a beast who worshipped a dragon would come up out of the sea and make war against the saints (Revelation 13). Guess what the Vikings had carved on the fronts of their ships...dragons!

Many church leaders were sure the Viking attacks were a sign of the coming of the end of the world. They believed this because Revelation also mentions a thousand-year reign of Christ, after which will come a new heaven and a new earth (Revelation 20 and 21). When Sweyn was born, the year 1000 was fast approaching--believed to be one thousand years after the birth of Jesus Christ.

However, the average person living in Europe at that time did not even know what year it was, and the calendar had changed a few times since the date assigned to the birth of Jesus. Also, most people had never read, or even heard, the words in the book of Revelation. The Vikings probably would have been very surprised to hear that they were supposedly mentioned in the Bible.

Most Vikings did not worship the God of the Bible like many of the people they raided. The warrior god Odin, "the all-father," was one of the Viking gods they followed. The Vikings believed there was great glory in winning battles and fighting well like Odin.

Long before Sweyn Forkbeard was born, the Danish Vikings had managed to take over and control the northeastern part of England. The section of England under Danish rule was called the "Danelaw." Of course, the English were not happy about that and kept fighting to get their land back. The Danelaw shrank or grew depending on which side won each battle. However, the Danes never put a king on the throne of England, until Sweyn came along.

*Ask your mom or dad what happened in the world when the year 2000 was coming.

4
Sweyn's Father

Sweyn's father, Harald Bluetooth, did not have a blue tooth. Bluetooth was a nickname for someone who had dark hair. Harald's hair was unusually dark, for a Dane.

When Harald was a young man, he and his older brother Knut went sea-raiding together. Knut was killed during an invasion of Ireland. Soon afterward, their father Gorm died from grief at the news of the death of his first-born son. Harald Bluetooth became the new King of Denmark.

While Harald was king, Earl Hakon, a nobleman from Norway who had lost his power and property, was living in Denmark. He helped Harald Bluetooth gain control of Norway by deceiving the King of Norway. King Harald then restored earl Hakon to power on condition that he would pay tribute to Denmark. So, Earl Hakon governed Norway for King Harald.

A few years later, Emperor Otto of Germany sent a message to King Harald. The Emperor said Harald must accept Christianity and be baptized, or else he would be attacked. The King sent for Earl Hakon and made preparations for war.

Earl Hakon and his men helped defend Denmark at the Danevirk. Emperor Otto gave up that fight and decided to cross a fiord to get his troops into Denmark. There he engaged King Harald in a fierce battle and won. Harald fled to a nearby island and decided to arrange a truce with the emperor.

King Harald was still reluctant to accept Christianity. He is said to have asked a church leader to prove his faith by putting on a white-hot metal glove. After the act was accomplished without harm, Harald was impressed enough to consent to baptism, and to declare Christianity the favored religion of Denmark and Norway. Emperor Otto also had young Sweyn baptized, and gave him the name Otto Sweyn. Now Harald

Bluetooth is called the first Christian King of Denmark.

After King Harald converted to Christianity, he ordered a memorial stone carved and set between the burial mounds of his parents. The famous Jelling Stone still exists. On one side is carved an image of Christ and on the other is a short biography of King Harald: "King Harald ordered theses monuments to be raised in honor of Gorm his father and Thyra his mother: the Harald who won for himself all Denmark and Norway and made the Danes Christian."

*Did you know that Bluetooth technology is named after Harald Bluetooth?

5
Sweyn the Son of Harald

Sweyn Forkbeard was not raised by his mother, who was a nobleman's servant, nor by King Harald, but by foster parents. Foster parenting was very common at that time, especially among the nobility. One king would raise another king's son, while someone else would raise one of his children. However, King Harald was not eager to claim Sweyn as his son, and did not want much to do with him. That is why he arranged for Sweyn to have foster parents.

At the age of 15, Sweyn bullied his father into giving him three ships and 100 men, which he used to cause mischief up and down the coasts of Denmark. He would twice more receive ships and men from King Harald, who hoped his son would finally be satisfied.

When Sweyn was about 20 years old, he went to his father and demanded to be given a piece of his father's kingdom. King Harald did not care for that idea and said, "No." Sweyn decided he was going to get what he wanted one way or another. He gathered all his ships and an army to fight against his father.

When Vikings fought each other, they often tied their ships together and fought right on the water. Then they would engage in hand to hand combat until one side was forced to surrender. Of course, King Harald was an experienced Viking who had fought, and won, many battles. Sweyn's army was not able to defeat his father's forces. So, instead of surrendering, Sweyn decided to turn his fleet around and flee.

After the battle, King Harald went ashore to rest. One of Sweyn's men found the king and shot him with an arrow as he warmed himself by a fire. King Harald died that very night. Sweyn Forkbeard became the next King of Denmark.

*King Harald's bones are inside a cathedral pillar in Roeskilde, Denmark.

6
Sweyn the King of Denmark

Before Sweyn officially became king of Denmark, he was kidnapped by some Viking warriors called the Jomsvikings. The Jomsvikings were a special group of strong, fierce, and courageous Vikings. They obeyed very strict rules and built their own fortress where they spent a lot of time training for battle.

The Jomsvikings told Swyen they would support him as King of Denmark if he would make a peace treaty with King Boleslav of Poland by marrying his daughter Gunhilda. Sweyn decided to do what they asked, so he went home to Denmark with a new bride. Gunhilda and

Sweyn eventually had five children: Harald, Knut, Gytha, Gunhilda, and Thyra.

As King of Denmark, Sweyn did not stay home and spend all his time sitting on a throne overseeing his kingdom. He loved the Viking life and led many raiding parties, most of them to England. Sweyn had big plans. He intended to become King of England! Perhaps Sweyn thought he could finish the job of conquering England that had been started by the Danish Vikings who went before him.

Coincidentally, in 989 C. E., people in England, and all over the world, were worried about the appearance of what we now call Halley's Comet. They believed it was a symbol of coming disaster, possibly even another sign of the end of the world. For the English people, their fears were soon realized in the person of Sweyn Forkbeard.

When Sweyn Forkbeard began his attacks on England, Ethelred the Second was King of England. Ethelred was about the same age as Sweyn, but he had become king at the age of eleven. Little Ethelred had not been ready to be king. Of course, since boys grow up to be men, he grew up too. Ethelred could have become a strong and courageous king. However, he spent most of his life being unready to defend his country from the attacks by Sweyn Forkbeard and his Danish Vikings, and so gained the nickname Ethelred the Unready.

Many times, King Ethelred submitted to King Sweyn's demands for tribute in order to buy peace for a while. Giving the Danes money became such a regular event that the money received its own special name: "The Danegeld."

The first payment of the Danegeld was 10,000 pounds of English silver in the year 991. Did that keep Sweyn from trying to conquer England? It certainly did not. Ethelred probably did not know that Sweyn had made a vow, in front of a bunch of friends, that he could take over England within three years.

7
Sweyn the Viking King

In 994, Sweyn and his friend, the Norwegian Viking Olaf Tryggveson, took 94 ships to England and tried to gain control of London. They were not successful, so they focused on raiding towns along the coast of England instead. Finally, King Ethelred offered to give them 16,000 pounds and feed their armies all winter, if Sweyn and Olaf would promise to stop the plundering. They promised. Olaf always kept his promise. In fact, he even decided to become a Christian and was baptized. Olaf eventually became King of Norway and never attacked England again.

Even though King Sweyn had been baptized as a child, he was not interested in Christianity.

He also was not interested in keeping any promises that he made to King Ethelred. In 997, Sweyn's Viking army resumed their attacks on England's coastal and riverside towns. They burned down many buildings and carried away everything of value.

King Ethelred and the people of England attempted several times to stop the Danes. However, almost every time they gathered enough men for an army, something would happen to keep them from being able to face the enemy. An army from Kent did manage to engage the Danes in battle but quickly gave up because they did not have enough help.

King Ethelred also tried to gather a fleet of ships together so he could defend the coastline. The ships he managed to get were never ready when they were needed, and the ships' crews became unhappy because of all the delays. Meanwhile, the Danes teased them by quickly attacking and then retreating out to the open sea.

The people of England began to be irritated with their king. So far every attempt to stop the Vikings was a waste of time and money. The Danes just seemed to be getting stronger and bolder.

8
What happened in the year 1000?

In Rome, on New Year's Eve, 999 C. E., crowds of people, along with Pope Sylvester the Second, gathered in St. Peter's Basilica. Others found their way to high ground, so they could be close to heaven when Jesus returned. Much to their disappointment, nothing happened. However, the year wasn't over yet.

All over the world in the year 1000, people kept busy just living their daily lives, without realizing that many important things were happening. Leif Ericson was busy discovering North America, the Chinese were inventing gunpowder, an Indian mathematician was learning about the importance of the number zero, the Mayans were reaching the peak of their civilization, and a poet was writing the epic called "Beowulf."

Sweyn Forkbeard was busy too. He was fighting a battle against his old friend Olaf Tryggveson. A woman named Sigfrid the Haughty provided the reason for the conflict. Sigfrid had been married to the King of Sweden. After the King of Sweden died, King Olaf of Norway proposed to marry Sigfrid, under one condition. She must give up worshiping the pagan gods and become a Christian. Sigfrid laughed. King Olaf, she said, could worship any god he chose, and so could she. She would not give up the traditional gods that were part of her family background. King Olaf became very angry and slapped Sigfrid across the face.

You have probably guessed that Sigfrid and Olaf never did get married. Can you guess who Sigfrid did marry? Sweyn Forkbeard! Gunhilda was no longer living.

Sigfrid was very bitter over the memory of King Olaf's insulting behavior, and she wanted revenge. She convinced Sweyn Forkbeard that he had many good reasons to go to battle against

Olaf. One reason was that Olaf had decided to marry one of Sweyn's sisters without asking for Sweyn's royal permission.

Another reason was that Olaf had been made King of Norway by the people of Norway. That doesn't sound so bad, but don't forget that Sweyn's father had once taken control of Norway and made it officially Danish. Norway had decided that Olaf Tryggveson should be its ruler. After all, he was the son of the former Norwegian King. This meant that Norway would no longer be under Danish rule. Of course, Sweyn did not like that.

Sweyn joined forces with King Olaf of Sweden, who was Sigfrid the Haughty's son, and Earl Eirik, the son of Earl Hakon who had helped Harald Bluetooth gain control of Norway. They found out that Olaf Tryggveson was going to make a sea journey to Poland. So they decided to pay him a surprise visit while he was there.

The three conspirators agreed to divide Norway into thirds if they could conquer Olaf Tryggveson. Olaf also had some extremely strong, beautiful war ships that they could not wait to get their hands on. Before those prizes could be won, hundreds of men had to lose their lives in a great Viking sea battle.

One of the men that died was Norway's King Olaf. He fought very bravely, but Earl Eirik and his men finally surrounded the king on his magnificent ship, the Long Serpent. Having nowhere else to go, he jumped overboard. He was never seen by his countrymen again. Sweyn Forkbeard gained control of a portion of Norway for Denmark once more.

So, the year 1000 came and passed. For a short time, England did not have to worry about the Vikings, and the end of the world did not come. A few Christians began to look forward to 1033 as the new date for the end of the world, supposedly 1000 years after the *death* of Christ.

9
Sweyn Forkbeard and Ethelred the Unready

As the years passed, the Danish Vikings continued to pester England with invasions; and in 1002, Ethelred gave them money again in agreement for peace. This time it was 24,000 pounds.

Soon after paying the Danes, King Ethelred became convinced that one day the Danes would kill him and have his kingdom. In order to prevent this, he ordered what is now known as St. Brice's Day Massacre. On that day, thousands of Danes living in southern England, men, women and children were put to death, including Sweyn Forkbeard's sister.

Now, no agreement, nor any amount of monetary tribute, could keep Sweyn from attacking England again. So, the burning, looting, and fighting continued. More and more of England came under Danish control.

In 1005, England was struck by a terrible famine. The Vikings, whose activities had probably helped to cause the famine, decided they would be better off in Denmark. They left England and sailed home.

The Vikings did not stay gone long however, and soon renewed their attacks on a weak and powerless England. Ethelred was advised to offer tribute for peace, again. In the year 1007, the Danes were given 30,000 pounds.

By now you should have noticed a pattern of events. Do you think the Vikings kept their promise of peace this time? If you guessed "no," you are right. It seems that Sweyn just could not resist the desire to conquer all of England. So back he went, again and again. By the year 1012, the Danegeld had increased to 48,000 pounds!

By that time, King Ethelred had certainly earned his nickname. He had not worked very hard over the years to protect his people or his land from Sweyn's armies. Whenever he did try to resist the Danes, or regain lost ground, his efforts were not very successful. The Danes now controlled almost all of England except one important piece, London.

London was very well protected, and had never submitted to the Vikings. Do you know why? The king lived there. If the king were to be killed or captured, England would be completely under Danish rule.

In the fall of 1013, Sweyn Forkbeard sailed up the Trent River in England. He met with very little resistance and was given horses and supplies for his army. The Vikings then rode toward London, making sure that every town along the way understood that Sweyn was in charge. The people of London, however, would not give in to Sweyn Forkbeard and fought fiercely.

Sweyn left London and camped with his army in the west, where many of the English nobility came to him agreeing to submit to his rule. Then Sweyn went back to his ships in the north, where he was greeted as King of England. Soon afterward, the people of London also gave in to Sweyn, because they feared him greatly.

What was Ethelred doing? Well, he was on a ship in the Thames River waiting for Sweyn to go away. He had already sent his wife and children to Normandy to stay with his wife's brother Richard, Duke of Normandy. When Ethelred realized that the whole population of England was willing to call Sweyn Forkbeard King of England, he decided it was time to leave.

History is full of kings who went to battle in command of their armies, and who fought courageously against their enemies, but Ethelred was not one of them. He ran away from England and went to live in Normandy with his family, where he would be safe. Sweyn Forkbeard declared himself King of all England.

10
Sweyn the King of England, Finally!

You can be sure that Sweyn forkbeard was very happy to consider himself King of England. It took longer than the three years that he had boasted, but he finally accomplished his goal. However, this chapter in Sweyn's life is very short. You will soon see why.

Legend says that one day Sweyn was surrounded by Danish troops, demanding tribute from an English town, when he was struck down by the ghost of St. Edmund. Edmund was a king of East Anglia who had been martyred by Vikings about 150 years earlier.

No matter how it happened, Sweyn Forkbeard died very suddenly in February of the year 1014. He was King of England for only a few short weeks. In fact, he is not even included in some historical lists of English Kings, because King Ethelred was still alive at the time. Poor Sweyn was soon forgotten. If you were to mention Sweyn Forkbeard to someone today, he or she would probably say, "Sweyn who?"

11
Sweyn's Son Knut

After Sweyn died, his oldest son Harald became King of Denmark. The Viking army decided that Sweyn's son Knut should become the next King of England. However, the people of England had submitted to Sweyn not Knut. Now they wanted to have their English king back.

Ethelred sent messages to his people saying he was willing to try much harder to rule wisely. He asked for their forgiveness and promised to forgive anyone who had previously acted against him, if they would all agree to support his return.

Ethelred's return was supported wholeheartedly. Word was sent out that all Danish kings would forever be outlawed in England. Ethelred gathered an army and successfully attacked the Viking supply town of Lindsey, before it was ready to respond.

Soon all of England was plunged into war. Some Englishmen became traitors and fought with the Danes. Some Danes fought for England because it was more of a home to them than Denmark. Others just fought for their own benefit, against Vikings or Englishmen. A few people switched sides frequently, depending on who was winning.

King Ethelred's successful return did not last. His rule over England was greatly weakened by all the turmoil. In 1015, he became sick and died. Ethelred's son Edmund was the new king of England.

Edmund was much bolder and braver than his father. He might have been able to vanquish the Danes completely, if some men he trusted had not betrayed him to Knut. Eventually, Edmund and Knut agreed to split up England between the two of them. Unfortunately, Edmund did not live long afterward. In 1018 Knut became King of all England.

The wars between Denmark and England were over for good. The Viking army was given a final Danegeld payment of 82,500 pounds, then sailed home to Denmark.

Knut ruled as a king of England for nineteen peaceful and prosperous years. His older brother Harald did not live long, so Knut also became the ruler of Denmark and part of Norway. He accepted Christianity and was such a strong and well-loved king that he is remembered as Canute the Great. Sweyn Forkbeard's name is now overshadowed by his famous son.

12
How Do We Know?

Almost all of what we know about Sweyn Forkbeard is from chronicles and sagas. A chronicle is a year by year written record of historical events. Sagas are long poetic stories that were told about the histories of families or kings.

None of the chronicles that mention Sweyn Forkbeard were written by Danes. Most were by men whose countries had been attacked by the Vikings. Some, like the Anglo-Saxon Chronicle, were recorded by many different people. Other chronicles were written by one man over the course of his lifetime.

Sagas were created as songs or poems that were memorized and recited over and over again.

Poets called skalds were often hired by a king to travel with his army and record, in poetic language, the events that occurred. Those events became part of a saga that was passed from person to person by word of mouth.

The people of Scandinavia (Norway, Sweden, and Denmark) have many traditional sagas. Very often hundreds of years passed between the time a saga was made up and the time it was written down. By that time, it had been repeated by hundreds of people, thousands of times.

Have you ever played the "telephone" game? If you have, you know that even one sentence can change a great deal after passing through just 10 people in a couple of minutes. That is why today's historians realize they need to use other types of information to confirm any facts mention in the sagas.

Archeological evidence, official records, genealogies, letters, and first-person accounts can help an historian decide whether an event or place in a saga was real or just slipped in to make it more poetic. Many of the details of Sweyn Forkbeard's life found in the sagas cannot be verified, but I have treated them as true in this account.

Bibliography

Brent, Peter, *The Viking Saga*, Nework: G.P. Putnam's Sons, 1975

Elton, Oliver, (translator), *Nine books of the Danish History of Saxo Grammaticus*, New York: Norroena Society, 1905; Online edition: Online Medieval and Classical Library, 1997

Hollander, Lee M. (translator), *The Saga of the Jomsvikings*, Austin: University of Texas Press, 1955

Ingram, Rev. James, (translator), *The Anglo-Saxon Chronicle*, London: Everyman Press, 1912; Online edition: Online Medieval and Classical library, 1997

Marsden, John, *The Fury of the Northmen: Saints, Shrines, and Sea-Raiders in the Viking Age,* New York: St. Martin's Press, 1993

Reston, James, *The Last Apocalypse: Europe at the Year 1000 A.D.*, New York: Doubleday, 1998

Sturluson, Snorri, *Heimskringla: History of the Kings of Norway*, Trans. Hollander, Lee M., Austin: University of Texas Press, 1964

About the Author

Angela Garcia lives in a small Virginia town with her family and Oscar the cat. She has homeschooled her five children over the last twenty-five years, with a focus on world history. Sweyn Forkbeard was researched and written over twenty years ago, for a children's history book contest. After it was not selected as the contest winner, it sat in a file cabinet waiting for the day it would be finally published.

Printed in Great Britain
by Amazon